Ordeal in Cambodia

Ordeal in Cambodia

One Family's Miraculous Survival —
Escape from the Khmer Rouge

A true story by

VEK HUONG TAING

as told to Sharon Fischer

Here's Life Publishers, Inc.
P.O. Box 1576 • San Bernardino, CA 92402

iii

ORDEAL IN CAMBODIA
Copyright © 1980 by Here's Life Publishers, Inc.
All rights reserved.
Printed in the United States of America
Library of Congress Catalog Card No. 78-78167
Here's Life Publishers Product No. 950154
ISBN No. 0-89840-007-4
Scripture quotations are from the New American
Standard Bible, Copyright © The Lockman
Foundation, 1960, 1962, 1963, 1968, 1971, 1972, 1973,
and are used by permission.

iv

Acknowledgements

I would like to express my sincere thanks to Sharon Fischer for her investment of many hours of helping me to write in English, and to Janet Kobobel for her editorial assistance in the refinement of the manuscript.

My gratitude also goes to Bailey Marks for his excellent contribution in the final editing of this book, and to the Here's Life Publishers staff, especially David Orris, for overseeing its production.

Dedicated to my beloved wife, Samoeun, who believed God with me for miracles during our four years under the communists in Cambodia. Because of her love, encouragement and prayers, I had the faith to trust God for miracles; and her support has helped me complete this book.

Foreword

At 2 a.m. in late April, 1979, my telephone rang. Bailey Marks, our director of affairs for Asia, was calling from the Philippines, and his message brought great joy to my heart and tears to my eyes. Vek Huong Taing, his wife, Samoeun, and son, Wiphousana, had been located in a Thailand refugee camp. No member of our staff had heard from the Taings since Phnom Penh, Cambodia, fell to the communists in April, 1975. The Taings were at that time serving in Phnom Penh as Campus Crusade staff members. After the city's fall to the Khmer Rouge, Cambodia was virtually cut off from communication with the outside world until the Vietnamese invasion of January, 1979.

When I learned that the Taings had been located, I reflected on a letter Huong had written to Bailey Marks in 1975, only 10 days prior to Phnom Penh's collapse. In the letter, Huong wrote of his dedication to helping reach his homeland for Christ, and expressed a willingness to die for his faith.

We had never given up hope that the Taings were still alive, though from what we knew of the conditions inside their country, it did seem that the odds were vastly against their survival. Thus, I was thrilled to learn that they were indeed alive and had escaped into Thailand. I was also sobered as I began to learn of the details of their four years under the Khmer Rouge regime, and was reminded of the very perilous times in which we live, as our freedoms, personal and national, are threatened on every side.

I commend this book to you, for it is an account of not only miraculous survival, but also of a courageous family's very special relationship with God, and how their faith sustained them and gave them hope in the midst of all but impossible circumstances. I hope and pray that this book will inspire and challenge you and, most of all, that it will be a vehicle to bring you into a fuller understanding of the love of God for all men, as demonstrated through His Son, Jesus Christ.

Bill Bright

President and Founder
Campus Crusade for Christ International

Preface

Cambodia has a long and rich history, and until the last decade it was known as a peaceful, gentle and fertile land. In 1970, however, that calm tradition was brought to a halt by the overthrow of Prince Norodom Sihanouk. Replacing Prince Sihanouk was General Lon Nol, Cambodia's premier under Sihanouk.

Sihanouk's overthrow had its roots in a centuries-old vehement animosity between Cambodia and Vietnam. The rebellious contingent of students and workers who overthrew the Prince were angered by his cooperation with North Vietnam in allowing supplies to be shipped to South Vietnam via Cambodia, a practice which let the communist North Vietnamese and Vietcong establish military "sanctuaries" inside Cambodia.

From that time on, the communists began to penetrate more deeply into Cambodia and, with the continued aid of the North Vietnamese, began to occupy village after village in the jungles of rural Cambodia, recruiting young troops from the peasant population as they went.

The Khmer Rouge (Red Cambodians), as this insurgent army came to be called, developed a drastic design for its revolution: the total abolishment of the old Cambodia, it's history, traditions, religion, government, military, and social and family ties. In its place would be the establishment of a peasant society, with all citizens engaged in agricultural production and all production belonging to the Khmer Rouge.

When the Khmer Rouge finally reached Phnom
Penh in April, 1975, they were ready to implement
fully their revolutionary plan, and they did so with a
barbaric brutality often likened to Hitler's Germany.

By 1978, Vietnam had turned against the Khmer
Rouge and its despotic leader, Pol Pot, and in turn
invaded Cambodia, thereby opening the country's
borders for the eventual escape of thousands of starv-
ing, disease-ridden Cambodians seeking release from
the Khmer Rouge regime. My wife, my son and myself were among those refugees.

Vek Huong Taing

Contents

The Fall

1

THE FALL

ON APRIL 17, 1975 Phnom Penh, Cambodia fell to revolutionary communism. The surrender of Cambodia's capital signaled ultimate victory for a guerrilla movement spawned in the rice paddies of rural Cambodia — a movement which in five civil-war-torn years had overtaken an entire nation.

The fall of Phnom Penh signaled something different for my young family and me, and seven million other Cambodians. Twenty-four hours after the city's collapse, my wife, our two-month-old son and I would begin a literal journey into the unknown. We would become exiles in our own country, stripped of everything but life itself. But we

4

would also discover an awareness of God in ways we never dreamed.

☆　☆　☆

The drive for communist control of Cambodia had begun in earnest in 1970. Outlying regions became the first battlegrounds for clashes between government troops and the Khmer Rouge, an army formed from Cambodia's peasant population and aided militarily by the country's communist neighbor to the east, North Vietnam.

By the end of 1974, the rural skirmishes had grown into full-scale fighting for control of Cambodia's major metropolitan areas. Almost every day in Phnom Penh, a public place such as a restaurant or cinema exploded in flames from bombs planted by the Khmer Rouge or from hand grenades thrown into buildings at random. The sky was constantly alight from bombs overhead, and the toll on human life was rising. Hospitals were overflowing with the injured and dying. Already the communists had sealed off major supply routes into Cambodia's cities, and they were closing down communication lines within the country.

Cambodia's economy was in upheaval, and inflation was running rampant.

As 1975 dawned, the political situation in Cambodia became even more difficult. Because of the frequent bombing around Phnom Penh, electrical power was sporadic at best and usually non-existent. Stores and shops closed down; frustrations were building in Phnom Penh's residents as they tried adjusting to the loss of a modern city's conveniences.

Samoeun[1] and I are native Cambodians, and we were serving then as staff members with Campus Crusade for Christ. We had just arrived back in Phnom Penh seven months earlier from a ministry training time in Manila, Philippines. We had thought through carefully that we were returning to a very insecure situation, but we loved our people and were fervent in our desire to share with them God's love and forgiveness through Jesus Christ.

We worked mostly with students at the University of Phnom Penh from which I had graduated a year earlier. I went on campus

---

1. Pronounced Sam-wän

7 April 1975

Dear Mr. Bailey Marks.

First of all we would like to ask your excuse by writing this letter by hand. As you know in this situation we don't have electricity to use our english electric type writer. within 48 hours we have electricity only 2 or 3 hours.

We just want you to know that we have received a check of 285.70 us $ for December reimbursement, but we could not cash it.

Now all classes are closed (college, High school, private school) we are making contacts at our place. The situation is very hard. we cannot say what will happen for next day, next week but we are happy to live and to die for our Lord Jesus Christ. No missionnary stay in Cambodia in this time and also some of our christian leaders want to run out from the country but for we both we have decided to serve our Lord Jesus christ until our last minute of lives in reaching Cambodia for Him. Please continue to pray for our strength both physically and spiritually. we do hope that if God's will we can see you one again before we die or we'll meet each other in heaven.

Please give our regards to all our beloved staffs of CCC around the world

Yours in our Lord Jesus Christ

Huong & Samoeun and be

Last word: Copy of letter sent by Vek Huong Taing one week before the fall of Phnom Penh.

daily to converse with students about Jesus Christ and to give spiritual guidance to those who had already placed their faith in Christ. At the university I found a spiritual hunger that was not there before the war had reached such proportions. Many students came to know Christ during those first few months.

In the beginning of March, top government officials began to leave Phnom Penh as the actual fighting approached the city limits. Many men were rushing their wives and children out of Cambodia while there was time, and several people who loved us much urged me to send Samoeun and our new-born son, Wiphousana[1], out of the country to safety.

Mindful of our friends' concerns, Samoeun and I prayed hard about what to do. As we thought of the enormous burden God had placed on our hearts for the Cambodians who did not yet know Christ, we decided together to stay in the country even though we knew how dangerous that would be.

---

1. Pronounced Wip-oo-sänä

8

On April 7, 1975, I wrote the following letter to Bailey Marks, the director of Campus Crusade's Asian affairs, in Manila, letting him know of our decision to stay:

Dear Mr. Bailey Marks,

First of all, we would like to [apologize for writing] this letter by hand. As you know, in this situation we don't have electricity to use our English electric typewriter; within [the last] 48 hours, we have electricity only two or three hours. . . .

Now all classes are closed (college, high school, private school). . . . The situation is very hard. We cannot say what will happen for [the] next day, [the] next week, but we are happy to live and to die for our Lord Jesus Christ. . . . We have decided to serve our Lord Jesus Christ until our last minute of lives (sic) in reaching Cambodia for Him. Please continue to pray for our strength both physically and spiritually. We do hope that if [it is] God's will we can see you once again before we die or we'll meet each other in heaven.

Please give our regards to all our beloved staffs (sic) of [Campus Crusade for Christ] around the world.

Yours in our Lord Jesus Christ,
Huong and Samoeun and baby

We sent our letter by airmail to Bailey, almost afraid to hope that it would ever reach him. By then the postal service was nearly non-functional, and the Phnom Penh airport open erratically. We wouldn't learn of the letter's fate for years.

☆ ☆ ☆

Just after we had mailed our letter off to Bailey Marks, life in Phnom Penh lost all sense of order and predictability. Whole families shuttled between homes of relatives and friends, as different parts of the city were transformed into war zones.

During this time I remained in close contact with my older brother, Chhirc[1], who worked in administration with the Lon Nol government in Phnom Penh as an army major. Chhirc had been a strong spiritual influence on me all my life, and his commitment to Christ remained firm as always. Recently he had had to make the difficult decision of sending his wife out of the country for her protection while he stayed in Cambodia.

In the days preceding the city's fall, Chhirc met early in the mornings with Samoeun and me to pray, and to discuss

------

1. Pronounced Chirk

Cheng Kdar
(sugar)
November 1976 —
January 1979

23 April 1979

THAILAND

LAOS

Sisophon
February 1979 — 21 April 1979

Battambang

CAMBODIA

Kok Trom (fish)
August — 15 October 1975

Pursat

Watt Kor
September —
November 1976

Norea
(coconut)

October 1975 —
September 1976

Phnom Penh
18 April 1975

VIETNAM

Takoa (food)
April — August 1975

Gulf of Siam

Don Ensign

*Four hard years: Map indicates approximate location
and dates of events during the Taings' ordeal.*

creative ways to witness for Christ in our difficult situation.

We finally decided to try holding a two-day training class in evangelism and discipleship for the university students with whom we had been able to maintain contact. The Takmoa Bible School, about six miles from Phnom Penh, was chosen as our site because it was presently removed from some of the main areas of fighting.

(It may seem that we were quite reckless to hold a training session under such violent circumstances. Although our intention was not to foolishly risk our lives or the lives of the students who volunteered to join us, we sensed that time was running out for opportunity to express our faith. We wanted to make the most of any options left. We didn't know, of course, how close at hand the city's collapse was.)

We scheduled our training institute for April 13-15, dates which happened to coincide with the Cambodian New Year. By the 13th, 100 students had registered for the training, and we all miraculously convened at the Bible school, having navigated our various ways through the hazardous streets and roads.

Unexpectedly, heavy fighting between government forces and the Khmer Rouge started up all around us as we began our class at the Takmoa Bible School. Midway through the first session, a Khmer Rouge cannonball exploded not more than 300-400 feet from our meeting place.

As I tried to continue on through the lesson, bombs were starting to fall around us like rain. Because many of the explosives were aimed for buildings, I decided we should continue on a grassy area just outside the meeting room. I instructed everyone to lie down on the ground, and we opened our Bibles to Psalm 91.

Trying to raise my voice above the noise and confusion, I began to read aloud the comforting passage, "He who dwells in the shelter of the Most High will abide in the shadow of the Almighty. I will say to the Lord, 'My refuge and my fortress, my God in whom I trust!' . . . You will not be afraid of the terror by night, or of the arrow that flies by day; of the pestilence that stalks in darkness, or of the destruction that lays waste at noon. A thousand may fall at your side, and ten thousand at your right hand; but it shall not approach you. . . ."

We prayed for God to take care of us, as **13**
He had just promised through His Word. As
we finished praying, we looked up and saw a
group of people running toward our area,
many wounded and bleeding and crying.
They represented a tiny segment of the
masses continuing to stream out of Phnom
Penh; some people on foot carried only their
essential belongings and some piled in cars
which were packed with as much as could
hurriedly be gathered.

Smoke filled the sky as factories went up
in flames and gas stations ignited in the
distance. I knew we had to move our group
back into the city. We had a shortage of cars,
and so we all moved inside the building
again to wait as trips were made back and
forth to transport everyone to Chhirc's
house. While we waited our turns to be
taken back into Phnom Penh our building
suddenly became the front line of fighting as
a Lon Nol tank discharged shells into one
section of the school, and the Khmer Rouge
returned fire.

Miraculously, we all made it safely in the
cars to Chhirc's house, which was located
across the street from Phnom Penh's Olympic Stadium, right in the middle of the city.

After everyone from the training seminar had gathered at his home, I brought Samoeun and Wiphousana from my house.

A large group of the students with families in Phnom Penh decided that they needed to reunite with them, but about 30 students, some who were attending the university away from home, remained with us to continue the classes. As the noise escalated around us, Chhirc and I decided to change the training program to a prayer program.

For the next 24 hours, we formed a "prayer chain" with our students, as it was almost impossible to sleep. Through the night the city sky was bright from explosions and burning buildings. Chhirc's house had a flat, patio-type roof, and often we prayed up there when we couldn't sleep. Our tears came down often as we viewed the destruction of our city and thought of the thousands of people dying without Christ.

At times we wondered if all we were witnessing might not be God's way of dealing with our land. Sadly, we recognized that our nation was corrupt; disrespect for the law was widespread, and the corruption in Lon Nol's administration was hardly a secret.

In our last ditch attempts to share the gospel, Chhirc suggested that we concentrate on government offices, located near his house. So from 6 to 8 each morning for two or three days, we dashed in and out of government buildings, distributing Christian booklets and stopping to discuss Christ whenever possible.

On the morning of April 17, we finished our pamphlet "blitz" about 8:30 a.m. As the students, Chhirc, Samoeun and I moved back toward the house, we looked up in the sky and saw a rapid volley of cannonball flashes going off in fireworks fashion, and realized it was the Khmer Rouge way of announcing victory. The insurgent army was now marching full-force into Phnom Penh.

We scrambled into the house. When everyone was in, I glanced out a window over to the Olympic Stadium, where the retreating Lon Nol forces had been bringing their tanks and artillery. From my vantage point I saw the white flag of surrender flying out of several cannon there.

I went over to the door and closed it. Chhirc and I asked everyone to sit down. On a blackboard we had set out for the training class, I explained to them the suffering that was now very likely to be upon us. I told them that we would probably all be separated soon and encouraged them to stand firm for our Lord Jesus Christ. I reminded them of the apostle Paul's words in Romans 14:9 that whether we live or die, we are the Lord's.

Many in the room began to cry quietly, as the reality of everything set in. After about a half hour of instruction and encouragement, I erased everything from the blackboard.

A few minutes later, there was a hard knock on our door. I opened it to a group of black-uniformed Khmer Rouge soldiers who ordered us to evacuate the house immediately and leave the city. We were some of the first Phnom Penh residents to receive such an order, because of our proximity to the city center and the government offices, where most of the soldiers had converged.

For the first few hours of the Khmer Rouge takeover, many other areas of the city were jubilant over the victory. To most people, it promised the end to civil war and the return of peace and stability. But joy soon turned to horror as the soldiers, without warning, spread their evacuation orders throughout the city of two million, allowing no time to contact family or friends or to gather personal belongings.

For us, when the soldiers moved on, we realized the time of our separation had come. The students wanted to make last frantic attempts to find their families or other relatives and friends, and Samoeun, Wiphousana and I needed to get back to our house. As tears came down again, we sang a song together about reunion in heaven, and then the students departed.

Not many people yet understood the kind of revolution fomenting, nor the totality of it. My brother, Chhirc, because of his access to classified government correspondence, comprehended the implications of this day more clearly than most.

As soon as the last of the students left, Chhirc took out his army identification card and tore it to pieces, knowing possession of it now would bring him certain death. As he prepared with us to run, he tucked his Bible under his arm and asked if we were going to accompany him. I felt it only fair to urge him to go on; my wife, baby and I needed to stay

18   together, and he might be able to move faster
fleeing alone.

Chhirc left the house, and I have not seen
him since.

The
Exodus

2

THE EXODUS

WITH Wiphousana in my arms, Samoeun
and I made our way through Phnom Penh's
turbulent streets to our home. We packed
urgently, though unsure of what to take. We
did agree to leave in our car rather than on
foot and to carry with us as much Christian
literature as possible as well as a supply of
powdered milk for Wiphousana.

I decided that we should hide in our
house for as long as possible, to see if we
could avoid the evacuation. After we
gathered our bundles of clothes, supplies
and materials, we crouched low in our house
to wait.

The victory the Khmer Rouge had now
secured was not bringing the random vio-

22

lence to a halt. As I peered out a window, right in front of our house a Khmer Rouge confronted a Lon Nol government soldier, asking him to remove his shirt and drop his gun. As the soldier did so, he was shot at point-blank.

We stayed hidden in our house through the morning and early afternoon of April 18. Around 3 p.m., I looked out behind the house and saw Khmer Rouge soldiers going from house to house, checking for inhabitants. I was able to observe the consequences of a resident's resistance: those who refused to leave their homes were being executed without hesitation.

We grabbed our belongings and jumped into our car. Crowds were still pouring through the city's streets; the Khmer Rouge were attempting to clean out the city literally overnight.

There were no exceptions to the rule. Hospital patients were thrown out into the fray along with everyone else. As we crept along the streets, patients rolled by still on their wheeled hospital beds, pushed along by relatives or friends. Many had tubes from intravenous feeding trailing from arms and legs.

Most of those patients would die within hours along the road; doctors and nurses had dropped many surgeries in process, caught up in the struggle for their own survival. We passed many pregnant women who were dying while giving birth along the road.

As for our little family, I drove our car slowly through the crowds, but I had no idea where to go. So Samoeun and I prayed, and asked God to lead us.

When we had left our house, two carloads of neighbors had left with us, and our three cars were trying to stay together as much as possible. About a quarter mile into our trip-without-a-destination, five gun-carrying men in Khmer Rouge black stopped our cars and asked to go with us. They told us that they would tell us where we should be headed, but their real intent was obvious as they eyed the few possessions we and our neighbors had packed in our cars.

When we were first stopped by the men, I wondered in the back of my mind why they had chosen us, out of all the hundreds of automobiles pushing their way out of Phnom Penh. I wondered if God might not have a plan for us in it all. I was soon to find out.

24   Though several of the soldiers had actually climbed inside the first two cars, the men with our car elected to ride on our hood as we drove. About one mile down the road, the lead car broke down. We all stopped as the five soldiers gathered around the first car and turned their full attention toward trying to fix it.

My neighbor in the second car got out and came over to me. We decided to try something risky. Our plan was to leave our families in our cars temporarily and disappear into the crowds, hoping that, when the soldiers realized we were gone, they would become impatient and abandon our group, not wanting to take our cars on ahead without the drivers.

When the first car was fixed, they turned around and looked for us in the crowd. We had hidden so that we could watch their actions; they waited for about 15 minutes and then all piled into the first car and drove on.

My neighbor and I ran back to our cars when the soldiers drove off. We found out the next day that the soldiers had taken our neighbors to an out-of-the-way spot and ransacked their car, stealing everything inside.

The forced exodus out of Phnom Penh continued, and the Khmer Rouge walked along beside the trudging crowds, keeping everyone moving. Whenever we asked our destination, we were told, "Far away! Keep going!" At night people slept under trees, in fields, along the roads. As the days wore on, we passed village after village with houses in shambles, and the sight of bodies strewn along the road became commonplace.

In spite of the chaos, young Wiphousana slept often and peacefully. Samoeun's delivery of our son two months earlier had been difficult, and some stitches had been removed by her sister just a week before Phnom Penh fell — it would have been hopeless to try having them taken out at any of Phnom Penh's overflowing hospitals. Samoeun was still bleeding sporadically from the stitch removal, and because of our car she was spared walking. I conserved on the gasoline supply by pushing the car on flat portions of the road and letting it coast down the declines of hilly sections.

As we continued on the road, we prayed often to God, asking Him again to lead us where we should go. After about two weeks of weary travel, we reached the Takoa Province and the village of Pey[1]. Takoa had been controlled by the Khmer Rouge for two or three years already, so most of the villagers had good relations with the occupying soldiers.

It was here in the village of Pey that I received my first introduction into the realities of our new life under the Red Cambodians. When I registered our name with the village leaders, we were questioned about our backgrounds, where we were from, who we worked for and how many brothers and sisters we had.

After I answered the registrar's questions, he asked me, "Did any of your brothers or sisters work for the enemy?"

I answered him, "What do you mean by 'enemy'? What kind of 'enemy' do you want me to say?"

The registrar then told me, in essence, that any professional person under the old regime — whether he worked in the military, in education, medicine or for the government — was considered the "enemy"

-----

1. Pronounced Pay

now. I had already heard via rumor that the Khmer Rouge were beginning a systematic slaughter of anyone associated professionally with the old Cambodia.

I knew I had to maintain my commitment to truth as I answered the man's questions, and so I told him of my brother Chhirc's occupation as an army officer. I silently entrusted my life to God, believing that if He wanted me to die simply because of my relation to Chhirc, it would only mean reaching heaven sooner and eternity with Him.

The registrar didn't react much when I gave him the information about Chhirc; he just wrote down everything I said. As we settled into the village, I would find myself being asked these same questions almost every day. And I would find out soon that Samoeun was being secretly pulled aside and asked the same questions that were asked of me — in an effort, of course, to see if our answers corroborated, thus making sure I was telling the truth.

On the evening of the fourth day after we had joined the village, all the "newcomers" were gathered together for a meeting with the village leader. There were about 100 of us there, and we shared one thing in common — we were all from cities and had been traumatically displaced by forced evacuation.

When Samoeun and I arrived in the meeting room, it was dark, with just one lamp flickering. Chairs had been pushed aside, and we were asked to sit on the ground.

To begin the meeting, the village leader asked, "Is there anything I can do for you?" One man stood up and said, "I have orders now to work in the fields far away from my children. They desperately need salt to go with their rice." (In Pey, our food each day was rationed rice mixed with water, making a thin, tasteless gruel.)

The Khmer Rouge leader replied angrily, "Why do you think we have salt? For years we have had to use ashes for *our* 'salt!' " In no less an angry manner, he then accused the entire group of being weak and soft because of our city upbringing. For most of us, that was the first time we would learn that being raised in the city was now a crime.

As our group heard the leader's harsh response to the request for salt, an atmosphere of fear invaded the room. The leader asked once more if there was anything we needed. There was no response, and the meeting soon ended.

Each village under Khmer Rouge control was broken down into groups, with a Khmer Rouge leader overseeing each group. In Pey, we were assigned to one group during our whole stay there, and for some reason our group leader took a special interest in us.

Samoeun was still bleeding sporadically, and so our befriending leader allowed me to perform my assigned job — hoeing land and planting vegetables — close to our make-shift shelter so that I could carry water periodically to my wife and Wiphousana from a well about 150 feet away.

He also took unusual compassion on me in regards to our daily food. Our portions of rice for porridge each day were not nearly enough to satisfy hunger; although the village residents were given plenty, the "newcomers" from the city were rationed strictly and meagerly. My group leader would often cook extra rice at his house for Samoeun and me, and after dark we would slip over to his house unnoticed and eat the extra nourishment.

As time went on, some of the longtime residents of the village also took an interest in us and gave us extra food. It was always done in secret, however, as they would sneak it up to our doorway when a Khmer Rouge soldier wasn't looking and run away. To be caught aiding newcomers in this way could mean death for them.

As well as being riskily generous with his rice, my leader friend also was generous with village secrets. For example, about three evenings after that first village meeting, another meeting was called for the newcomers. In this meeting, the village leader asked everyone who had been an officer in the Lon Nol army to write his name on a list, and then head back to the fields and rice paddies to his work. Told that the list was being compiled to start sending people back home to Phnom Penh, the newcomers obliged with happy surprise.

But my group leader had told me that when the former officers returned to the fields that night, death was awaiting each one at the hands and knives of the Khmer Rouge. The next morning, other workers were welcomed to their day's work in the rice paddies by the bodies of the officers floating in the water. The purge of the "enemy" I had previously heard rumored was now proven fact.

My leader also let me in on another secret: Khmer Rouge agents were routinely hiding beside our shelter at night, listening in on private conversations between Samoeun and me to catch anything that might further incriminate us as city people. We heeded the warning well; but it was difficult to believe that not even the night time could provide a haven from the ever-present Khmer Rouge.

In an effort to emphasize our need for wariness in what we spoke even privately, my group leader took me secretly a few times to a mountain near our village, less than a mile from my shelter. There he would show me the deposited bodies in shallow mass graves of those newcomers who had already been spied upon and found guilty of often nothing more than city-dwelling. The smell from the mountain was overwhelmingly bad, and occasionally it wafted down into the village, serving as a sharp reminder to me to proceed about my daily life with the utmost caution.

After two or three weeks of living in Pey, Samoeun and I realized how limited our chances were to talk to others about our faith in Christ. Besides the uncertainty of not knowing if any given conversation was being monitored, there was no time to serve God. Each day I worked from 6 a.m. to noon, then from 1 p.m. to 6 p.m. and from 8 until night's darkness fell. We prayed that, if we were to go on living, we would be brought out of the captivity of the Khmer Rouge's Cambodia and into a place of true liberty in order to serve God fully.

So we asked God to pave the way for us to leave Pey and somehow get to Battambang, a province near the Thailand-Cambodia border. Perhaps if we reached Battambang we could escape across the border into freedom.

Then, about four months after we had arrived in Takoa Province, the leader of my group asked me to begin packing our things; the Khmer Rouge were moving all the newcomers to new locations.

I asked him where we would be going. He told me the group was being divided and would be sent three different places — one of which was Battambang.

One
Fish
a
Day

3

ONE FISH A DAY

WHEN the day came to leave Pey, all the newcomers were gathered together. We were instructed to walk down a road for about six miles and wait there for a truck which would take us to our new destinations. Samoeun and I discovered that God had a plan even in the timing of our departure — Samoeun's bleeding had completely stopped, and she could now handle the walking.

Our group arrived at the designated truck-rendezvous site and spent two nights there, waiting to leave. There were about 30 trucks parked in a large area, and hundreds of people milling around, because the make-shift way station was not only for our village but also for many other villages around.

When we were ready to leave, the Khmer Rouge unexpectedly asked us to deposit all our belongings on the ground beside the road before we climbed aboard our assigned trucks. A great cry of shocked protest went up from the crowd, but soldiers promised over loudspeakers that we had no cause for worry; all we needed would be taken care of by the Khmer Rouge.

Not completely trusting the soldiers' reassurances, hundreds of people began frantically piling layers of clothes on their bodies, knowing they could only take with them what was on their person. Quickly the Khmer Rouge dispersed through the crowd and, using their guns as goads, began pushing everyone up onto the trucks. We were loaded on, about 90 people per truck, and even though we were all standing, our bodies were pressed together with no room to spare.

After everyone had been packed on the trucks, we gazed out the sides only to see the soldiers voraciously rummaging through the possessions that had been left by the road, taking freely that which they wanted.

At this, many of the helpless captives on the trucks broke out in angered sobs. Samoeun and I had peace, though our hearts hurt too, only because we had truly given everything we owned over to God and knew that if all our material things were taken from us we still had Him. We felt most deeply for the hundreds of anguished people without Christ, whose hearts were in those possessions left on the ground.

As the trucks rolled out, none of us knew where our particular vehicle was headed. Samoeun and I prayed silently that if God's plan was for us to eventually serve Him freely, He would direct our truck to Battambang.

Not long after we had left the truck way station, we came to the outskirts of Phnom Penh. I could hardly believe that it was once a thriving city of two million; it was literally deserted now. Where before busy crowds had filled the streets daily, now only one or two Khmer Rouge soldiers sauntered by, guarding the emptiness. Our truck moved by the University of Phnom Penh, where I had studied and where our Campus Crusade ministry had begun. In place of the beautiful flowers and trees that once graced the front of the university, rice paddies now sat as practical reminders that this communist revolution had uprooted things of beauty for the sake of productivity.

Presently our truck passed the French Embassy and took a road whose signs pointed to Battambang! When everyone in the truck saw we were headed to the "near-border" town, a collective cheer arose from the group. Battambang, because of its location, now signaled potential freedom for every Cambodian. As our truck rumbled down the road, Samoeun and I smiled at each other, believing God had answered our prayer to remain alive and serve Him more fully. After one more night of travel, we stopped in a town named Pursat.

At Pursat, we were instructed to climb off the truck and transfer to a train. As we stepped off the truck bed, a Khmer Rouge soldier in charge of the transfer came up to me and began asking questions which were by now familiar: my name, my former profession, my brothers' and sisters' jobs. I wondered, why had the soldier singled me out of the crowd? Was I being chosen to be killed?

But believing that God would take care of me, I answered the questions honestly.

After I answered, he said to me quietly, "For some reason, I feel concerned about you and want to warn you not to take the train to Battambang. You are being lied to — you'll never reach Battambang's main city, or even outlying villages, but they'll drop you off in the jungle, and you'll die of starvation."

Then the soldier offered, "Listen, why don't you stay here with me? We have plenty to eat — I'll list you in the village as my brother and sister."

I had to make a difficult decision on the spot. It seemed God was leading us to Battambang but here was an offer for security and protection. I thought quickly, but in my heart I knew I had to follow what I believed to be God's will, by faith. I thanked the soldier profusely for his kindness, but said that I felt we must go on. As Samoeun and I stepped aboard the train, the soldier shook his head, and as his eyes followed me, they were filled with sadness, communicating fear of what might lie ahead for us.

The decision weighed heavily on my mind, because I could not ignore the kind soldier's warnings of the suffering we might encounter. But I believed that God would

40

work His plan out, and I was sure I had done the right thing.

The train pulled out of the station, and about 18 miles before Battambang City, the province's main town, the train stopped suddenly at a tiny station. At that point, the Khmer Rouge ordered everyone off the train — and told us we were to be left there, just as my soldier friend had predicted.

The area was thick jungle. Bare vestiges of civilization could be seen, such as an occasional thatched roof in the distance, mostly created by people who had been deposited from trains just as we had, but months before. Our train had been filled with weary Cambodians, most of us born and raised in cities such as Phnom Penh. Now we had reached the climax of the communist plan for us — to be stripped of everything we had known or could lay claim to from our former lives.

As the emptied train pulled away, men, women, and children began to sob. Despair cast a pall over the entire group of 300 people, as the hopelessness of trying to imagine beginning anew in such surroundings was contemplated.

It was about four p.m. when the last of us

touched the ground and the train steamed off. The sky was darkening, and it looked like it was about to rain. The monsoon season was upon us, and the chilly air penetrated our worn clothes. No one had a coat to protect himself either from the chill or the impending rain.

Samoeun was holding Wiphousana, and as she looked up at me, her tears began to fall. She sobbed into my arms and couldn't say a word, but I knew the fear overwhelming her — what to do about the rain, and how to protect Wiphousana. I prayed once again, giving the whole situation over to God and asking Him to take care of us.

After we stood there for a little while, a man emerged from a path coming out of the jungle near us. He came over to me and said, "I really feel sorry for you — it's about to rain and you have no protection. Why don't you come and stay in my shelter tonight, and tomorrow you can build your own?" I found out that he had been living in the jungle only a month and had come to the tracks when he heard a train coming. Our new friend led us back on the path through the thick trees and brush to a small Khmer Rouge-controlled settlement called Kok Trom. We stayed with him that night, and over the next few days I fashioned my own shelter out of the jungle's bamboo and brush.

Even though our new "home" was deep in the jungle, the Khmer Rouge controlled the area as tightly as any place we had been. There were soldiers everywhere, surrounding the area, guarding every possible escape route with an immediate sentence of death for each fugitive.

Kok Trom was organized in typical Khmer Rouge fashion, with a village leader, group leaders and a communal kitchen. When we first arrived, the Khmer Rouge fed us about as much rice per day as could be contained in a small milk carton. About a week later, this was reduced to half that much, and a couple of weeks later, our daily ration was just about what a soup ladle can hold. Not only did such a small amount of rice do more to whet an appetite than satisfy it, but our portion was not guaranteed daily. Some days the soldiers simply chose not to feed us, and there was no option but to hope there would be food the next day.

Hunger took its toll on everyone, in one way or another. Even in such a tightly controlled setting, a black market flourished, and I remember the day that Samoeun and I were so hungry I stealthily made it out to a road where I traded with a man my gold wedding band for eight oranges.

Others lost more than wedding rings, as starvation claimed its victims day after day. Malaria also took many lives. One of my jobs for awhile was to bury those who died each day. Sacred ritual was abandoned as each person was wrapped in his clothes and put in a shallow grave, shallow only because we didn't have the physical strength to dig deeper.

As time went on, Samoeun and I became concerned over the lack of nutrition Wiphousana was receiving, since our small daily portions of rice often could be supplemented only by boiled leaves and grass. Though Wiphousana was small even for his six months, due to a lack of proper vitamins, he had not fallen seriously ill. This was remarkable considering the inadequacy of his meager diet and the fact that all day long he was exposed to the dust and germs of primitive village life. So we prayed and asked God to show us how to make up for the things his diet was missing.

My main job, along with most other vil-

44

lagers, was planting rice. Most of each day we would plant, but I was finding I had some spare time each day in the paddies. One day I thought, "Why not try fishing for Wiphousana in the paddies during my spare time?" It was really a laughable idea, because the largest fish ever seen in the shallow waters was two to three inches long at the most.

But the first day I tried it, I caught a fish that was 8-10 inches in length — a catch unheard of in those paddies. And every day for the next two months, God provided a fish about that size — just one fish every day. Others noticed my success and tried catching fish that size too. But no one ever caught anything other than the small ones always found there. So in that way, God met the special needs of Wiphousana for a period of time.

After two months, it became harder and harder to catch fish; I began to wonder if God was holding back my daily provision for a reason. Samoeun and I realized that we could not stay much longer in Kok Trom and remain alive — death could come soon by starvation if by nothing else.

We discussed together what God's will

for us might be, and then I felt impressed to make a very specific request of God: we decided we would know whether or not to leave Kok Trom if someone came to our shelter and said, "Do you want to go out with me?" We didn't know who that person could be; we just felt that's how we would know God's leading.

After about a week of praying, no one had yet come to our shelter with the words we were looking for. Our tears began to flow as we were growing more and more hungry and had no place to turn for help.

In our area there was a young man named Kheang[1] whose family lived in Battambang Province. Kheang had been studying in Phnom Penh, though we had never talked much with him. One day, Kheang slipped over to our shelter and whispered to me, "I want to rejoin my parents in Prek Luong (a village in the province). Do you want to go out with me?" Samoeun turned to me, incredulous. "Did you hear what Kheang said to you?" she asked. We laughed

---

1. Pronounced Kăng.

quietly but joyfully at such specific answer to prayer and without hesitation said yes.

Kheang already had an idea for our escape, but before we discussed the plan, I told Kheang about the way he had been an answer to prayer. Then I shared with our new friend my faith in Christ, and how Kheang could come to know Him too.

I explained to Kheang God's love for man, but that man's sin separates him from knowing God personally. I went on to tell him that God sent His own Son, Jesus Christ, to pay the penalty for sin on the cross. By placing faith in Christ for salvation, I said, Kheang could know that his sins were forgiven, and he would establish a personal relationship with God and have eternal life. Kheang responded eagerly that he would like to become a Christian.

Then, after rejoicing together over his decision, Kheang and I decided to make our escape attempt the next day, which was October 15, 1975. Our plan was to steal out of the area very early in the morning before the village guards took their posts and run to the little train station, about a half mile away. Kheang knew when a train usually came by, and we hoped to sneak onto a car as the train slowed down.

Very early in the morning on the 15th, Kheang, Samoeun and I crept out of our village, with Wiphousana in my arms. It had begun raining the night before and had just stopped as we left our settlement. The train track was located across a large field of rice paddies, and because of the hard monsoon rain, we had to wade through waist-high paddy water to reach the tracks.

That day, no train came by. One guard passing by asked where we were going. We told him we were just going down the road to work. He shrugged and moved on. Later that evening, he came by again and asked us why we were still there. Samoeun told him that because of our baby, we were hoping the train would give us a lift to our work place. He shrugged again and walked on by.

That night it began raining again. For a moment, we began to question if we were doing the right thing; if maybe we shouldn't go back. We were soaking wet, tired, cold and hungry. But as we thought about the rain, we realized it was God's way of protecting us — monsoon rains are so heavy that one can hardly see ahead when they are coming down. The rain prevented the Khmer Rouge from coming to look for us.

In the morning, we came to a decision point: should we try to go on? Many obstacles lay ahead, and if we met the Khmer Rouge now, we would be killed. We decided unanimously that God was leading us to Battambang, and as soon as we all agreed to continue, a surge of strength swept through each of our weary bodies.

We began to walk down the tracks, and five miles later we reached another train station, this one slightly larger than the one near our village. A guard at the station asked me where we were going, and if we had permission, reminding us that those caught traveling without a Khmer Rouge permission slip were often killed on sight.

I replied to the guard that we didn't have permission, but it really didn't matter, because if we tried to stay in the jungle we would die anyway. Samoeun rather boldly suggested, "If you just give us permission, we won't die!"

At Samoeun's remark, the guard just shook his head and didn't seem to know how to respond. The Khmer Rouge had woven such a spell of fear over the Cambodian population that most people were afraid to look the average soldier in the eye, much less be so outspoken as Samoeun.

During this discussion, a train pulled into the station. We wanted to break and make a run for a car, but we quickly observed that the train was filled entirely with Khmer Rouge soldiers!

The guard with whom we had been talking looked at us and said, "What are you going to do *now*?"

Suddenly a soldier jumped off one of the cars and ran over to us. It was the soldier who in Pursat had warned us about taking the train to Battambang! As he ran toward us, he called out to Samoeun, "Sister, sister! Where have you been?"

When he reached us, we told him we had been in the jungle and everything had happened just as he said. Then he glanced over at the soldier guard and told him we were his relatives. He gave us his ID and a permission slip, and we climbed on the train with him. We received a lot of strange looks, because our dress was quite different from the black-suited Khmer Rouge. But we rode on to Battambang in safety — and wonder.

The
New
Cambodia

THE NEW CAMBODIA

THE TRAIN eventually brought us to the city of Battambang, and we got off at the city's large train station. As we walked across the station platform, we saw that, like Phnom Penh, Battambang was largely deserted except for a few Khmer Rouge soldiers. Most buildings were destroyed, and everywhere we looked there were cars piled in heaps. The cars themselves did not look badly damaged, but we noticed almost all of them had been stripped of their tires. We found out later that the Khmer Rouge made sandals out of the tire treads, discarding the otherwise useful automobiles into mountains of metal.

Our soldier friend had introduced himself to us on the train as Mao, and he brought us to a home which housed the family of a Khmer Rouge soldier. There Mao fixed us a full meal of rice. It was the first time since we had entered the jungle that our hunger was abated.

After dinner, Mao asked me where I wanted to go. I told him I had no idea, so he suggested the village Norea. He had heard that in Norea people were treated well and had enough to eat.

Norea was about six miles away, and it was a good feeling to walk confidently down the road, waved through guard stations easily as we flashed Mao's ID claiming us as his relatives.

After about an hour's walk, we arrived at Norea. Kheang left us there, borrowing Mao's identification card to get to his family's home about two miles from Norea. He told us later what a joyful reunion it was, since the family didn't expect to ever see him again.

Kheang's family had established good relations with the Khmer Rouge and thus had been able to keep their beautiful home. Kheang told his family all about us, and later we would occasionally receive permission to visit with his family. When we did, they always fed us well and provided us with fresh clothes. And when Kheang came to see us, his family would generously send along clothes, medicine and even cooking utensils.

After Kheang left us that first day at Norea, Mao introduced us to the village leader with whom we registered our names as new residents. As we waited for our work assignments and other information, I took a moment to reflect back on God's faithfulness to us in the past few days — sending Kheang to us and arranging our arrival at the train station to coincide with Mao's. God had indeed planned ahead, bringing us the right people at the right places and times. Even when we had foreseen countless obstacles back at Kok Trom, He had prepared our way. Now we were in Norea, at least a few steps closer to the freedom for which we had prayed.

During our first two months at Norea, the whole village was fed well. We were even given the privilege of cooking our rice in our huts rather than eating communally.

But the picture soon changed for the 388 of us residing in this village. The Khmer Rouge decided suddenly to require village

members to cook and eat in a central area.
They went from shelter to shelter and hut to
hut, confiscating all the rice in the village. If
someone was discovered holding some rice
for himself, he was severely beaten.

Under the new plan we received only a
soup-ladle-sized portion of rice per day.
Within a couple of months under this new
system, people began dying of starvation or
contracting diseases such as malaria, their
bodies especially vulnerable because of
malnutrition. The Khmer Rouge provided
no medicine or medical facilities; any such
treatment was devised by individuals from
roots and other parts of the plentiful banana
trees around.

After working all day, we often labored
on into the night, shelling rice by hand. The
Khmer Rouge had destroyed all the machin-
ery formerly used for such basic procedures,
in order to fill our days and nights with hard
physical labor. Our minds had no time to rest
or reflect and therefore evaluate objectively
all that was happening to us. The discour-
agement to think was also one purpose behind the scant portions of food given to us —
the Khmer Rouge understood well that a
hungry man is more interested in filling his

stomach than he is in intellectualizing about his surroundings.

Besides the hard work and meager food rationing, the Khmer Rouge used another technique in trying to keep us from pondering our situation. This technique was psychologically one of the most difficult adjustments Samoeun and I had to make: a complete communication cut-off from the outside world.

Not only had the Khmer Rouge impounded all radios they could find, but all books, magazines, newspapers and letters were seized, and no one was granted access to reading material of any kind. We were also denied writing paper and pens or pencils. This banishment of the written word extended far beyond the individual Cambodian: I learned later that in 1975 entire city and university libraries had been burned to the ground, leaving in ashes much of the documentation of a nation's culture and history. That was precisely the motivation behind such destruction: after all, a *new* Cambodia had come.

One reason for the Khmer Rouge's almost unthinking destruction of culture and history is that its ranks were composed mainly of young men from Cambodia's peasant population who had never received any formal education. Many of the soldiers along the roads were boys of 12 or 13 years of age, and aside from having had no schooling, until they became soldiers, many had probably never been more than a few miles from home.

By recruiting both uneducated men and unschooled boys, the communist infiltrators into Cambodia were able to indoctrinate an army well and thoroughly in revolutionary ideology, and instill in their recruits a fearful suspicion of the "oppressors" from the big cities.

The young communist soldiers also learned quickly to follow orders without question, and I knew that much of the Khmer Rouge's brutal, random killing was done without reflection or remorse — the soldiers saw themselves as simply carrying out orders.

At Norea, we had just as little to eat as anywhere we had lived, but God met our needs in an unusual way again, just as He had with the daily fish catch at Kok Trom. There were many coconut trees in Norea, and one day the village leader told me that if

I could climb the trees and retrieve coconuts for him during my free time, I could keep one for myself each time as payment.

The first time I tried to climb one of the limbless trees, I slid right back down, my chest bleeding as it scraped against the rough thin bark. But I kept trying, catching on in a short time, and for some reason I soon became the village leader's favorite climber. From my coconut payments, Samoeun and I were able to mix the coconut meat with our rice porridge to add some nutritional value. The coconuts were also considered valuable currency, and occasionally I traded them secretly for medicines and fish.

I had another need which seemed impossible to have met in our primitive circumstances: before the Khmer Rouge capture of Phnom Penh, I had slipped and fallen, breaking four of my front teeth. Though I had them capped before the fall, after about six months in the jungle the caps had broken off. I had wanted to have them fixed, but had given up hope that it could ever be done.

Kheang knew that I needed my teeth fixed. So one day when he came to visit, he whispered to me that his mother knew a former dentist from Battambang who was now a peasant in a village across a nearby river. Kheang said his mother also needed her teeth fixed and had received permission from the Khmer Rouge to cross the river. When he asked me if I would like to go with her, I could hardly refuse.

I knew that my teeth work would probably require several trips, and I would have to sneak out of the village unseen to make them. The dentist also would have to perform the work without being discovered, so Kheang's mother and the dentist arranged for all of us to meet for several successive days during breaks from planting rice or during lunch and dinner, when we would least likely be missed.

At my first meeting with the dentist, he told me that I was very lucky; after fixing Kheang's mother's teeth, the material he would use for me was the very last of the supply he had brought out of Battambang. After about a week of our meetings, the dentist had replaced my four front teeth, without benefit of any modern equipment such as an electric drill. In payment I gave him my watch — kept hidden since we left

Phnom Penh — my last possession of any
value.

Since we began living in Khmer Rouge
villages, I had observed the fear and suspicion that enveloped the lives of people who
were placing their hopes in their hidden
wealth. As I thought of my sale of my wedding band for eight oranges and the yielding
up of my watch for dental work, I knew I had
to be careful to keep placing my trust in our
Lord, not in my possessions which could become so relative in value.

Under the communists, when someone,
like the dentist, received gold, jewelry or a
watch in trade for food or for a service ren-
dered, the recipient's first priority was to
keep the payment hidden from the all-seeing
eyes of the Khmer Rouge. When the Lon Nol
government fell, the conquering army seized
as many valuables as possible from their
captured countrymen, explaining that everything would be used ultimately to help
"build the nation's economy." They were also
trying to reeducate a nation into thinking
collectively; i.e., the individual owns nothing, but everything is shared equally by all.

This reeducation was as forcefully carried out as everything else was, and if

62

someone's secret valuables were uncovered by the Khmer Rouge, it was an offense punishable immediately by death. The Khmer Rouge also had undercover agents pose as peasants occasionally to catch illegal trading in action and bring justice quickly to the offenders.

The communists had a saying, "If we cut down the tree, we must remove the roots." One sure means of "rooting out" the undesirable elements in the new society, such as hoarders of money and personal possessions, was the flourishing Khmer Rouge "accusation" system. This system provided a means of gaining favor with the communists, whereby the more people you could accuse — and the more things you could accuse them of, such as laziness or disloyalty — the higher you rose in the eyes of the village leadership.

Accused people were usually brought before the village in a twice-weekly evening meeting, called a *"kô sang."* Here a person's charges were announced, and he had an opportunity to admit his guilt. Normally one's second appearance at a *kô sang* guaranteed death; sometimes just one appearance was sufficient for the Khmer Rouge. (One reason for the *kô sang* ritual was that when an admission of guilt was elicited, the Khmer Rouge could then say that the offender had felt unworthy to be called a communist and had requested to die.)

At Norea the death sentences were carried out on the nearby river's bank, and the usual method of killing was a hard blow to the back of the neck with a bamboo stick. The bodies then fell into the river, saving the Khmer Rouge the trouble of burial. When I came to Norea I remember sometimes hearing, from a distance, voices screaming, "What's wrong with me? What did I do wrong?" I learned later that the voices were those of people who had been hit but were not yet dead. I remember the outcries for help, for someone to save them, and then there would be silence.

It was also a potential capital offense to put up protest or show emotion when a family member or friend was executed. To the Khmer Rouge any display of feelings evidenced sympathy with the accused person's attitudes, and therefore made the sorrowing survivor vulnerable to accusation himself.

Accusations became everyday occurrences in the new Cambodia, and it was not surprising to see an atmosphere of suspicion pervading life, dividing friends and family. Neither was it unheard of for husbands and wives to bring their spouses to be accused in the *kô sangs*, as the communists sought to abolish all personal loyalties so that one's only emotional ties were to communism. Not only were husbands and wives set against each other, but also as the Cambodian population settled into the new communist villages, all children above the age of eight were forcibly segregated from their families to areas near their home villages. They were allowed to visit with their parents occasionally but spent most of their days becoming indoctrinated in revolutionary thought and working their own rice paddies and vegetable patches.

Because of the innumerable and unexpected things that could warrant accusation, our city backgrounds and education were enough in themselves to make Samoeun and me very cautious. Since Samoeun and I had to be so careful, we could say nothing to our co-workers about our Christian faith. But about one month after we arrived in Norea, some people from my village group said to me, "Huong, you seem different from other people here. You've never accused anyone to the Khmer Rouge; and if someone is doing something wrong, you talk to them secretly about it. We've seen you on your break time helping some of the older people carry water."

I suppose those things were noticeable to my co-workers only because each person's work was very hard and there was little energy left over to help others. Their comments enabled me to tell them quietly, on our short breaks or as we chopped grass or tilled the land, that any love I displayed came from Christ living within me. As I told my friends how they could have a personal relationship with Jesus Christ, some were afraid to begin following Him, knowing that under the Khmer Rouge it could cost them their lives. Most were more interested in getting enough food to eat than in thinking about God. But two of my co-workers at Norea eventually did become Christians.

Our ministry as we had known it in the "old Cambodia" with Campus Crusade for Christ was obviously curtailed, but Samoeun and I found one thing we could do consistently, if secretly: pray. At Norea we began praying every day for the strength and growth of Christians around the world, and for each staff member with Campus Crusade whom we had met during our training in Manila. And we prayed that some day we would be reunited with our staff family to continue the work in freedom to which God had called us.

☆ ☆ ☆

After 11 months at Norea, the food situation was getting harder and harder to take. We weren't getting nearly enough to eat to sustain life much longer. So one morning Samoeun and I prayed to know God's will for us next. We asked Him to show us that very day if there was a way to escape from Norea. Then we went off to work and to wait for God's answer.

Hopes
and
Disappointments

5

HOPES AND DISAPPOINTMENTS

IN OUR village group at Norea, Samoeun and I had come to know a Chinese woman, Mrs. Chhuy Ngeang,[1] whose husband repaired cars for the Khmer Rouge in Battambang. Occasionally she was given permission to visit him.

During one of Mrs. Ngeang's visits to Battambang she had met a leader in the Khmer Rouge named Him Sarom[2]. One day, in the course of conversation, she told Him Sarom about us and about our Christian faith, mentioning our training with Campus

---

1. Pronounced Choy Nyang   2. Pronounced Him Sar-ŏm

Crusade in Manila, and about our desire to get out of Cambodia. Secretly, Him Sarom had replied to Mrs. Ngeang that he was not in agreement with the Khmer Rouge revolution and that he wanted to escape the country too. He told Mrs. Ngeang that he considered us his friends, even though we had never met.

In the afternoon of the day that we prayed to know God's will about leaving Norea, Mrs. Ngeang slipped us a letter from Him Sarom. The letter read:

> To Brother and sister Huong and Samoeun,
>
>   I left Cambodia to Thailand ahead [of you]. I was in a hurry. I could not bring you along with me. We are brother(s) and sister of one Heavenly Father, though we [do] not know each other. . . . I know how much you want to get out, but don't worry. Someday I will come back and bring you out, or send someone to bring you out. God bless you.
>
>   Him Sarom

After reading Him Sarom's letter, Samoeun and I agreed that it was God's answer to our prayer. Even though we had not yet met our new friend, we felt it was God's will to wait for His plan.

Our relationship with Mrs. Ngeang continued to grow, and often I shared coconuts with her and her three children. One day, Mrs. Ngeang told me that she was going to seek permission through her husband in Battambang to leave Norea for Watt Kor, a village to the north where she had heard food was more plentiful. She said that she would seek permission for us also, claiming us to be her relatives. Since Mrs. Ngeang knew I was a Christian and because I had shared with her the miracle that had brought us from Kok Trom to Norea, she asked us to pray for a similar miracle as she sought permission to leave Norea.

Soon after Mrs. Ngeang requested permission, she received a letter granting all of us the opportunity to leave for Watt Kor. It was amazing to receive such permission — it almost seemed as if it would be easier to go from one country to another than from village to village under the Khmer Rouge's Cambodia. Even if someone had heard word that his parents, living in another village, had died, he would not have been able to go bury them; the Khmer Rouge felt it would be a waste of time. Going to see a dead body would not raise it to life again!

Not only was it unusual to receive permission so easily, but it was also not common to receive an accompanying letter. Usually the Khmer Rouge province leader just gave a spoken yes or no. When I showed our letter to the village leadership, they were extremely surprised, having never seen permission by letter.

About one month after Mrs. Ngeang and her three children and Samoeun, Wiphousana and I arrived in Watt Kor, we met a woman who had escaped from Norea. She told me, "Huong, you are very lucky. After you left Norea, the Khmer Rouge executed everyone who had either worked for the Lon Nol government or had been a student during his regime."

Samoeun and I joyfully thanked God for leading us out safely, but when we told Mrs. Ngeang how God had worked, she suddenly became very angry. She told us that we had no right to thank God when it was she who was responsible for saving our lives. She said that many people had offered her gold to help get them out, but because she cared for us she chose to help us, though we had nothing we could offer for payment. Now we had turned around and thanked God instead!

We tried to explain to Mrs. Ngeang that we hadn't meant to exclude her from our appreciation but that she could feel honored because God had used her in such a special way. But her anger smoldered, and within a day or two she had gone to the Watt Kor village leaders, telling them that we were Christians, that we worked for an American organization (another crime worthy of death) and that we had received training in Manila.

We learned later from an acquaintance of Samoeun's in Watt Kor that when the village leader heard Mrs. Ngeang's accusations, he communicated them to the Khmer Rouge official responsible for ordering executions. The agent contacted one person in the village who knew us before the country's fall: a Lon Nol army pilot's widow who was a classmate of Samoeun's during high school days.

Samoeun's classmate gave the official a very favorable report about us, denying we had ever exhibited disloyalty to the Khmer Rouge or loyalty to western influences. The agent believed her and dropped the charges.

A few weeks later, the Khmer Rouge asked Mrs. Ngeang to return to her husband in Battambang. As she left, she told

Samoeun and me that she would be going immediately to the highest Khmer Rouge officials in Battambang with her accusations against us — and recommend us to be killed.

Meanwhile, as had happened in each previous village we lived in, our food rations were progressively cut back. Soon we had very little food. My family had a little relief for a while; one man who was responsible in his group for catching fish would secretly bring us a few fish every day before he took the rest to his group.

Wiphousana was now a year and seven months old. Samoeun's job in Watt Kor was to grind rice in a mill, and she was able to keep Wiphousana with her as she worked. My job was cutting bamboo; those of us performing that task were transported by truck for a couple of weeks at a time into a jungle area only 10 miles from the Thailand-Cambodia border.

When I first learned about my job I vowed to Samoeun that, even though we would be working so near the border, I would not think of escaping without her and Wiphousana. I assured her that if one day I didn't return, she would know I had been killed by the Khmer Rouge or died from a disease in the jungle. There was no medicine provided if we fell ill, and one of our co-workers had already died of malaria during one of our two-week stays.

Two months after we had moved to Watt Kor, I heard it announced that 30 families were to be moved from Watt Kor to a village called Cheng Kdar[1], four miles away. All we knew about Cheng Kdar was that it had been established recently and already had a reputation for severe strictness and little food. The people of Watt Kor became very upset at this news, dreading the thought of being sent there.

When Samoeun and I heard the news, we committed the situation to God. A few days after the announcement the list was announced, and we were named among the families chosen to leave. There was much anxiety about the move on the part of most of those chosen, but Samoeun and I felt peaceful, believing that God would care for us.

Everyone's fears about Cheng Kdar proved to be justified. We were worked

---

1. Pronounced Chĕng Kädär

harder there than at any place we had been so far and once again had very little to eat. We were not allowed to catch fish for extra food or keep for ourselves vegetables we might grow near our place, planted on work breaks. If fish or vegetables were found hidden in our huts, it would mean certain death.

Our "home" in Cheng Kdar was a tiny room in a small house that had once been occupied by Buddhist monks before the accompanying pagoda was razed by the Khmer Rouge. Several families occupied the cramped dwelling. It was Khmer Rouge policy here to deny families any sense of privacy so that we would be more aware of things we could accuse each other of.

Our work schedule carried us from sunup to sundown, and our strength began to drain away. If we became too sick to work, the Khmer Rouge would accuse us of being lazy, taunting that if we could walk and eat, surely we could work!

For awhile, Samoeun and I gained some relief from the meager diet. At Cheng Kdar one of the group operations was the making of sugar from the sap of palm trees. Not long after we arrived our group leader asked me to help him, secretly and on my free time, with the sugar mill's accounting and paperwork. In return he secretly gave me palm juice and sugar every day, and told me I could have some any time I wanted. From that sugar, we found enough extra nourishment to get us through each day with increased stamina.

Fear of the Khmer Rouge was intense in Cheng Kdar. Suicides became a frequent occurrence as the weeks and months went by. Many husbands deserted their wives when a chance for escape came, and from their despair some of the abandoned wives hanged themselves. Severe psychological depression had taken root as most people became totally apathetic about tomorrow — never knowing if they would be alive to see it. For Samoeun and me, we had, out of necessity, become apathetic primarily about our bodies, having long since given up bathing, combing our hair or brushing our teeth.

At Cheng Kdar, we had opportunity quietly to share our faith in Christ with about 10 or 20 people, and one of our co-workers committed his life to Christ. When we talked with these people, we not only shared with them God's plan for salvation, but also told them as much as we could about how to grow spiritually, knowing that if they became Christians we had no way to continue to help them to grow.

Many times we asked God, "Why, when we want to serve You so much, do we not have the chance?" When we became discouraged about our ministry limitations, we would often review in our minds a talk from our Campus Crusade training, "How to Rest in God's Plan." Recalling this message helped us to remember that God had a special plan for us, and we could rest in His revelation of it step-by-step.

Almost as a symbol of my faith I had kept my Campus Crusade ID card secretly, since Takoa, hoping that if we reached the border it could be shown to a journalist or someone who could then inform other Campus Crusade staff that we were still alive.

Samoeun's job at Cheng Kdar was to help clear out the jungle areas for planting rice. She would often hum softly to herself as she worked, and at times would sing songs in English that we had learned from our training in Manila. She had no idea that anyone could hear.

On her lunch break one day, after she had eaten, Samoeun's group leader, Ann, brusquely told her that she was being summoned into a *kô sang,* convening immediately. Samoeun's heart was pounding as she came into the meeting, and she tried to recall what she might have done wrong.

Once inside the meeting room, she was surrounded by Ann, the village leader and some of Ann's assistants. Then Ann started the accusations, calling Samoeun "lazy," insisting that even though Samoeun was physically strong many of the older women outworked her. Samoeun was also accused of singing "imperialist" American songs and being a secret member of the U.S. Central Intelligence Agency. Ann's assistants repeated the accusations, and Samoeun was warned that a second *kô sang* would mean death.

By the time the group had finished accusing Samoeun, her tears started to flow. But she kept quiet, knowing that if she tried to defend herself against the charges, the group would only intensify the accusations.

Back in our little room where Samoeun and I usually met after lunch to visit until our lunch break was over, I began to worry. Presently Samoeun came into our room, and when she saw me she burst into tears.

I became very anxious inside when she started crying, out of fear for what she had to tell me coupled with concern that a neighbor would see her crying and accuse her. But I comforted her, and as I wiped away her tears, Samoeun told me what had transpired at the *kô sang*.

After she had told me the whole story, I said to her quietly, "Samoeun, we must not be angry with the leaders. We have God, so let's pray now." We stole behind our house to a place hidden from everyone's view. We began to pray there, asking God to take care of us and to forgive Samoeun's accusers. We prayed especially for Ann that she would become Samoeun's friend.

Not long after Samoeun's *kô sang,* Ann's husband, who had been a government worker under Lon Nol, and one of his friends, a former professor, came to me secretly. They told me that because of my ties with Campus Crusade, an American organization, I was sure to be killed soon. They asked me if I would like to escape with them. There was a condition, however: if I agreed to go, I couldn't bring my family.

I refused their offer, and soon after I talked to them, I learned that they had escaped, leaving their families, including Ann and her two children, behind.

After her husband left, Ann became very frightened that the communists might accuse her of harboring disloyal attitudes. She was afraid, too, for the safety of her children because they were still small. One day, as she and Samoeun walked out to the fields together, Ann suddenly broke down. She told Samoeun how depressed and alone she felt since her husband left. "Every day my heart is so sad," she cried. "My life on this earth is nothing. If I wasn't afraid for my children, I would take my life today."

Samoeun whispered to her, "Ann, I have had many upsets and sad things happen. But I have peace in my heart because of Jesus living in me." Samoeun then told Ann how she could come to know Christ too. When she finished, Ann was very quiet, and after a long silence, she wiped her tears from her eyes and walked on ahead of Samoeun to work.

☆　☆　☆

Because of my educational background, my city upbringing and my ties with the western world through Campus Crusade, I was looked upon with great suspicion at Cheng Kdar. Following my position as an "accountant" with the village leader at the sugar mill, I was moved down the job scale. For an entire year my chief responsibility was to gather all the villagers' excrement for use as fertilizer in the village's agricultural endeavors. I was not given a shovel for the job, but a narrow board, and since I had not used soap since we fled Phnom Penh, I'm sure Samoeun's marriage commitment to me was tested often during that year! During my whole time on that job, a Khmer Rouge officer was assigned to watch me constantly, which may have been a wise idea: escape seemed very attractive to me many times that year.

The official's purpose, of course, in such close surveillance was to find something I could be accused of. But after I had been at the excrement job for a year, the village leaders apparently began to trust me, and I was given a new job, that of teaching the village's children to read.

I became a teacher in name only, because the children were allowed only five hours of instruction per week. The rest of the time I was responsible to oversee them as they worked in the fields. Then, not long after I began teaching, I was asked to become a leader of 10 village families.

I was very surprised when they asked me to become a group leader, because usually that job was given only to those who had been peasant workers before Cambodia's fall. I even protested the appointment on that basis, but the village leader wouldn't let me say no.

I enjoyed being a group leader, especially because the job left me time to care for Wiphousana. At that time Samoeun was often gone two weeks at a time planting rice some distance away, and though I had to work, too, I was able to keep Wiphousana with me.

I also enjoyed being a group leader because, in some ways, I was able to lead the group as I chose. I had the authority to give my group their allotted days off, and I made certain that they got them consistently. One day, after I had decreed a rest day, Ann, who was in our group, said to me, "Huong, the love you have for us is a very good love!"

As a group leader I also gained some popularity because of the way I conducted the group meetings required every three days. Instead of holding accusation sessions, I used the time to teach my group as much as I could about patience, love, kindness and other Christ-like character qualities.

One day, near the end of 1978, Mrs. Ngeang, the Chinese woman who had left us in vengeful anger at Watt Kor, suddenly appeared in our village. She had come to look for me, having heard that we were living a good life, relatively speaking, at Cheng Kdar, and that we had food to eat.

I was shocked when I saw Mrs. Ngeang; her head was swollen and she was extremely thin, obviously suffering severely from malnutrition. Mrs. Ngeang told me that the Khmer Rouge had killed her husband, having suspected him of working with the Vietnamese who had been threatening an invasion of Cambodia.

Because of my position as a leader, I was able to give Mrs. Ngeang all the extra food I could — potatoes from our small private garden and sugar from the mill. As we expressed kindness and acceptance toward her, she asked us our forgiveness for the attitudes she had held toward us. She noted sadly that she had indeed wanted the Khmer

Rouge to kill us, but instead they killed her husband.

We wanted Mrs. Ngeang to stay at Cheng Kdar, but our village leader would not grant her permission. So we gave her as much extra food as we could gather, and she left, returning to the village from which she had come.

Near the end of December, 1978 the Vietnamese invaded Cambodia.

Edge
of
Freedom

6

EDGE OF FREEDOM

BATTAMBANG, only nine miles from Cheng Kdar, was one of the first Cambodian cities attacked by the Vietnamese. A few days later we learned that when the news of the Viet invasion reached Watt Kor where we had lived before Cheng Kdar, the Khmer Rouge wiped out almost the entire adult male population. The soldiers claimed that all the men were secretly loyal to the Vietnamese. The men who did survive were forced to run for their lives, deserting their families. I realized that if we had stayed in Watt Kor, I might have had to do the same.

I also learned from my village leader at Cheng Kdar that I was on a master list of people to be killed soon. The list had been sent from Battambang and was drawn up arbitrarily by top Khmer Rouge officials based on the urban backgrounds of those "selected" for it. Had Vietnam not invaded Battambang and forced the Khmer Rouge officials to flee, I probably would have been executed sometime in January.

When the Vietnamese invaded the country, most of the residents of Cheng Kdar escaped into the mountains to hide — not so much from the Vietnamese but from the Khmer Rouge. In a panic spree of terror, gangs of Khmer Rouge soldiers were storming through villages, killing wantonly for fear that villagers would soon join hands with the Vietnamese forces.

Most people from Cheng Kdar fled to a mountain area about two miles behind the village. When rockets started to fall on our hamlet, Samoeun and I snatched up Wiphousana, grabbed a large bag of rice and ran.

As we were heading up into the hills, Wiphousana, now four years old, asked me, "Do we go to our Lord's house now?" I smiled a little and said, "No, we're going to the mountains."

(We prayed with our son often, and many

times he would sing prayers we had taught him as he played. He would sing in both Khmer and English, but because he couldn't speak well yet, no one but Samoeun and me could understand him. That was fortunate, for at times he would sing out, "Lord, let us out of here! . . . ")

Five families fled Cheng Kdar with us, including Samoeun's former accuser, Ann, and her two children. That night we hid together in the mountains with rockets exploding overhead all night. Ann and her children had caught up with us as we hurried into the mountains, and that night, as we all huddled together, she expressed how glad she was that she had found us. Samoeun couldn't resist saying, "Yes, Ann, you are very lucky! I have one more chance now to share with you about Jesus Christ!" That night Ann and two others in our group, a widow and her 18-year-old daughter, invited Jesus Christ into their lives.

After we prayed, Samoeun said to Ann, "I am so happy that you know Christ now. I prayed a long time ago that you would become my friend." Ann asked Samoeun if together they could forget the accusations Ann had made. She said the Khmer Rouge actu-

ally had asked her to make those charges —
and she was afraid for her own life if she
didn't comply.

We stayed near the mountains for about
three days. We could tell that the Khmer
Rouge were losing to the Vietnamese; from
our hiding place we could observe Khmer
Rouge soldiers shuffling by, most with severe wounds and carrying themselves with a
defeated bearing.

Our group still had rice to eat but had
run out of water. We decided to try going
back to Cheng Kdar where there would be a
water supply, since it seemed that the
Khmer Rouge had been driven out. We
moved down the mountain to an area close to
the village where other villagers were waiting, also pondering their next step.

When the other residents found out we
wanted to go into Cheng Kdar, they shook
their heads at us and warned us of the
chance we were taking. But our group of five
families prayed together about the venture
and agreed to go on in.

When we arrived in Cheng Kdar it was
silent; a strange contrast to the noise and
activity of normal life just a few days before.
Many houses and shelters were destroyed

and bodies were strewn throughout. An occasional hand grenade dotted the ground. We felt uneasy about staying there, so we headed out of town to the main highway that ran throughout Cambodia. Thousands of Cambodians, "freed" from the clutches of the Khmer Rouge by the Viet invasion, filled the highway.

Vietnamese soldiers were abundant on the highway also, and we were instructed by them to move quickly on the road to Battambang, because the Khmer Rouge were still fighting. Demolished army tanks and trucks from both sides of the conflict sat beside the road as we filed along, and it seemed that people were coming from all directions heading toward Battambang.

We arrived in Battambang that night, having walked about eight miles in a day. Food was scarce, and many people who ventured into hopefully abandoned villages to search out bags of rice were killed tripping land mines left by the Khmer Rouge to hinder just such activity. Some Khmer Rouge soldiers were also hidden around the villages to shoot returning scavengers on sight.

In Battambang, we happened across Mrs. Ngeang, our Chinese friend again. She

94

seemed very happy to see us and said she had been looking for us since the Viet invasion. Then she suggested that if we wanted to get out of Cambodia, we should go with her to Sisophon[1], a city about 37 miles north of the city of Battambang. Mrs. Ngeang was sure we could get across the border from there. When she mentioned Sisophon, Samoeun and I thought back to the letter she had given us from the Khmer Rouge soldier Him Sarom. Perhaps we could contact him from Sisophon.

We could not travel very fast to Sisophon because of the children and because of the need to be cautious about the possible presence of the Khmer Rouge along the way. We asked news of villages up ahead from other travelers to check on the safety of passing by the villages. At night we slept under trees and beside the road along with many other people. After three days of walking, we reached Sisophon.

Naturally we wanted to continue on the road to the border, but the Vietnamese had sealed off the road. So we had to set up

---

1. Pronounced Sis-o-pŏn

"camp" near Sisophon. We were in a relatively dangerous place. The Khmer Rouge who were still alive or uncaptured entered villages and continued their rampage of killing.

The Khmer Rouge were also known at that time to round up people found hidden in the jungle or outside villages and, with a long needle and thread, string villagers together through their hands and lead them into the nearest hamlet. People who refused to allow this to be done were usually shot.

Near Sisophon I built a shelter for us all near a Vietnamese army camp, located about 600 feet away. We were soon joined at our site by Mrs. Ngeang's sister, whom she had just found (they had been separated since the fall of Cambodia) as well as her sister's husband and their little son. Two young men also joined us, Savonny and Ratha, who was a Christian. Our group now numbered 25. As we waited there at Sisophon, I had much time to converse with different members of the group about Christ's love for them, and during our days there, 10 people became Christians.

After several days at Sisophon, the 25 of us became anxious to make a move for the border. Everyone in the group had by this time made a commitment to Christ, and so one day we all prayed together for God to reveal to us the next step. After we prayed, we decided to choose Mrs. Ngeang to be our chief strategist: besides her Chinese language fluency, which would be useful in relating to many of the Vietnamese troops, she was, though temperamental, a very friendly person by nature and met people easily. We prayed for her as she went out into Sisophon, asking God to lead her way.

A few days later, Mrs. Ngeang met in Sisophon a Vietnamese army officer who had known her sister in Phnom Penh. The officer and Mrs. Ngeang's sister had studied communism together secretly, but in 1975, when he saw the extremes to which the Khmer Rouge were going to enforce the doctrine, he escaped to Vietnam and joined the army there.

Mrs. Ngeang related to the officer the suffering she had endured for four years under the Khmer Rouge and told him how much she wanted to escape to Thailand. She mentioned there were 25 people in her group and asked him if he could help. The officer agreed to help prepare the way for us since he was also aiding more than 100 Thais who had been trapped inside Cambodia. However, there was one condition: Mrs. Ngeang and her sister must promise to work for the communists in Thailand after they crossed the border. Mrs. Ngeang at least tacitly agreed to his condition.

The Vietnamese officer then introduced Mrs. Ngeang to other officers who were secretly involved in getting people safely across the border. The officers asked her to give them our names and then she returned to our camp to tell us the good news.

That night we divided into small groups to pray for the continued success of our mission. I noticed quickly that Mrs. Ngeang refused to join in our prayer and became concerned that she might be getting upset, as she had in Watt Kor when she felt slighted because of our focus on God.

One day, the Vietnamese officer gave a letter to Mrs. Ngeang, written in French. In the letter he said that he had made contact with Vietnamese across the border, and they had agreed to help us come out. The letter then mentioned the man who would meet us in Cambodia and secretly lead us out. His name: Him Sarom.

After Mrs. Ngeang showed me the letter and I saw Him's name, I wanted to jump for joy. I thought back to his letter to us in Norea in 1976, and felt that God's hand was in our efforts. That night I asked everyone to pray again for God's further leading.

It was very obvious by now that Mrs. Ngeang was upset again. As everyone else was praying, she took me aside and said, "Huong, why do you need to pray? If I hadn't gone to seek a way for us to gain permission, you never would have received it! Would God have found permission for you without me?"

Mrs. Ngeang stalked off, and the next day she came up to me to tell me that she had found another group of people who wanted to escape. She said that these people were able to pay her in large amounts of gold and other valuables for her knowledge and the contacts she could make.

Mrs. Ngeang then told me that she would be making her escape attempt eventually with the new group and offered to take us along. After thinking about her offer, I decided to discuss it with the members of our group, even though for myself I knew I would not be going with her.

That same day another offer to escape came our way. About two months before, Ratha, one of the young men who joined our group at Sisophon, had introduced me to a Christian woman named Mrs. Phalla,[1] also staying in Sisophon. Mrs. Phalla had been anxious to meet us, having had no contact with other Christians during her four years under the Khmer Rouge. During the intervening two months, Mrs. Phalla introduced us to 18 of her relatives who were staying with her, and each of these family members became Christians. Our two groups visited frequently at our shelter site, and it was refreshing to be able to freely follow up their decisions for Christ by teaching Christian songs and helping them learn the portions of the Bible we had memorized before Cambodia's fall to the Khmer Rouge.

On the day I decided to part ways with Mrs. Ngeang, Mrs. Phalla came to my shelter. She had come to say goodbye, because she and her group would be making an attempt the next day to reach Thailand. I asked Mrs. Phalla how she was making the

---

1. Pronounced Fǎllǎ.

trip — by herself, or was she paying a guide?

Mrs. Phalla said she would be paying a guide, and when I asked what it cost for each person, she answered that it was $350 in gold. My heart sank at that figure, because I knew I had no money for myself, much less anyone else. She also mentioned that her guide did not want to lead a very large group through the jungle, and in addition to the 18 people in her family there were two more nephews and another family who had asked to join her. Samoeun and I prayed with Mrs. Phalla for God's blessing on her journey, and she turned to leave our shelter.

A few steps later, Mrs. Phalla stopped. She turned around and said she'd just thought of something: Why not send two people from our group along with hers to learn the way? Then those two would return to bring us out the same path. My spirit brightened at the new proposal, and I told Mrs. Phalla that our group would be meeting that night and I would present her idea, letting her know of the decision early in the morning.

Our group met that night as planned, and took votes to see who would be leaving with Mrs. Ngeang and who would stay with us. When we took the vote, 11 people chose to go with Mrs. Ngeang, and six out of our original 25 decided to stay in Sisophon a while longer, making other arrangements later for their escape attempts. That left eight of us ready to escape as soon as possible.

After the meeting adjourned, our new group of eight met together and appointed Savonny and Ratha, the two young men, to scout out the trail with Mrs. Phalla's party.

Early in the morning of April 21, Savonny and Ratha crept out of our shelter area over to Mrs. Phalla's. About an hour later Ratha came running back. "Huong," he panted, "Mrs. Phalla asked me to tell you that the other family in her party plus the two nephews decided not to join her. She has invited all eight of us to come, and she will pay the guide enough for each of us!"

Within minutes we had all gathered our things and were slipping quietly away to meet Mrs. Phalla.

A little after 7 a.m., April 21, 1979, we all prayed together and then started off toward the border.

Even with our guide secured, success couldn't be guaranteed: the only possible escape routes were through thick, uninhabited jungle, and the guides, no matter how large their payment, could never be totally trusted not to abandon their groups in the midst of the bamboo forests, slipping away with gold in hand. Some guides were actually secret Khmer Rouge agents who would murder their charges deep in the dense wilderness.

It would be a venture of faith.

Escape!

7

ESCAPE!

AS OUR new group of 26 stole away from Sisophon, we separated into smaller groups so that we wouldn't be identified as exiting the city all together. After a day's walk we came to an isolated village. We were about 15 miles from the border.

The village was very quiet, and it looked like possibly 20-30 families lived there. We stopped briefly to rest and then moved on through the night. On the morning of the 22nd, we stopped again. At our resting point, we prayed hard, asking God to take care of us the rest of the way. We were now entering the densest jungle area and many unknowns lay ahead: the possibility of a surprise Khmer Rouge attack, a sudden hostile reac-

tion from patrolling Viet soldiers or aban-
donment by our guide.

After our rest, we continued on. The
journey's complications were increased by
the six children with us. Two children
needed to be carried, and four needed to be
held by hand. If we came upon the Khmer
Rouge, we wouldn't be able to run.

The jungle vegetation was so thick that
no path was recognizable. Small bamboo
plants with sharp points stuck up from the
ground everywhere, and our bare feet began
to bleed. Along the way we frequently saw
bones from human skeletons, and the smell
of death was in the air. As we came closer to
the border, we passed by broken-down au-
tomatic bow-and-arrow machines, which
were undoubtedly in full working order
when the Khmer Rouge ruled Cambodia and
could be much more protective of the border.

We walked along silently, afraid to make
a vocal sound lest any stalking Khmer
Rouge should hear. As we came within three
miles of the border, we were all ready to give
up. Most of the women could barely take
another step, and the children could not
keep their tears bottled up any longer. Worst
of all, our water supply was depleted.

We stopped once again and wearily decided to pray. We quoted in our prayer from Psalm 23, "The Lord is my Shepherd, I shall not want. He leads me beside still waters . . . ." Then we asked God to meet the needs of our thirsting group. After we finished our prayer, two or three men went on ahead. About 160 feet beyond us they all converged on a small hole practically hidden from sight. Normally the small hole would have held no water, but rain from the night before had filled the hole.

The men called out their discovery, and we all joyfully raced to the hole and luxuriously drank until thirst was quenched. Then we filled all the jugs and small barrels we carried and, expressing our thanks to God, moved on with renewed strength.

On the night of April 22, our guide stopped us in the middle of our path. "You are in Thailand now," he said, and just as quickly vanished into the thick brush.

Momentary fear swept our group, because the night was pitch black, and we had no way of knowing in which direction lay a village, if indeed we had crossed the border.

But once again, we sat everyone down to pray. We asked the Lord to be our guide since

we had no human guide anymore. We
finished praying and got up to continue moving in a westerly direction. But it was so
dark we couldn't see where we were going
and decided to stop where we were to sleep.
That decision in itself was an act of faith,
because even in the darkness we could detail
the footprints of tigers and other wild forest
creatures.

Just as we were ready to go to sleep, I
asked two young men in our group to climb
the nearest tall tree to see if they could see
any village lights. When they came down
from the tree, they told me they saw two sets
of lights, one set near and one set farther
away. I asked them to remember the direction, and we would head that way in the
morning.

As April 23 dawned, we aroused from
sleep and started moving in the direction of
the lights the men had seen the night before.
As we passed through the jungle, we came
upon the wheel tracks of an oxcart probably
used to haul chopped wood. Upon seeing this
sign of civilization our pace quickened
considerably. About two miles further we
passed a group of people planting rice. Just

beyond them lay a village. We knew for certain we were in Thailand.

As we approached the village, a Thai soldier greeted us. He asked us how we had gotten out of the forest, and since I didn't know the Thai language, I answered him in English. He seemed excited to find an English-speaking Cambodian, since he spoke both English and French, and we established an immediate rapport. After asking about our experiences in Cambodia, our new friend warned us not to go into the nearby refugee camp, because the Thai government was planning to send refugees right back into Cambodia, without food or protection. He invited us instead to his place for the night.

At his house, the Thai soldier fed us well, and as he and I talked further that night, he offered to find a job for me in the village — which would give me the opportunity to resettle quickly and avoid the uncertainties of the refugee camp. I then told my friend about my work with Campus Crusade and my intense desire to resume contact with the staff. He replied that I would probably have a better chance through the camp of contacting outsiders than by staying in the village.

So on the morning of April 24, the Thai soldier led us into the refugee camp. The camp was obviously makeshift and hurriedly constructed. Barbed wire formed its borders, and the housing consisted of long rows of roofed shelters without walls.

As we arrived in the camp, we were met by many of the residents, who expressed surprise at how physically strong we looked. But they were most surprised that our entire group of 26 had made it. We were told that every group which had arrived so far had lost members in the jungle. The refugees mentioned one group in which only 10 people ultimately reached the camp out of an original 60.

During our first week in the camp, called Taphraya[1], we took the opportunity to share with many people how they could come to Jesus Christ personally. Nineteen refugees became Christians that week, and each morning and evening I began holding a Bible study for them and for other Christians who wanted to join. Thailand missionaries also visited the camp, and it was

---

1. Pronounced Tä-pry-ä

exciting for me to see Christian literature and Cambodian Bibles freely circulating.

During our first days in the camp, we spent much time wandering through the rows of shelters, looking for someone, anyone, we might recognize as a Christian whom we had known before the fall. We looked particularly hard for any Thailand Campus Crusade staff who might be visiting the camp. The camp had now swelled to at least 75,000 people, and I knew it would almost be a miracle to ever meet anyone.

I remember one evening as Samoeun and I wandered through the camp on our search for familiar faces, we noticed a man who looked like a member of the Red Cross. He very closely resembled a Campus Crusade staff member we had known in Manila, Bud Newbold. Samoeun ran up to the man, her heart filled with optimism that we had found an old friend. But about one or two feet before she reached him, she looked more closely and realized he was not Mr. Newbold. Samoeun's disappointment was so immense that she fell to the ground before him, crying.

As I circled around the border of the

camp two days after our arrival, through the barbed wire I noticed a Caucasian newspaper reporter standing just outside the fence. Reporters were not yet allowed inside, and their interviewing had to be done through the barbed wire. A crowd was gathering by the fence where he was standing, as any reporter represented in everyone's mind a slim ray of hope that he might convey a short message that would reach relatives in the outside world.

As I joined the crowd, I heard the reporter calling out above the noise for anyone who knew English to come forward. At this, my heart started pounding, for it was becoming obvious that I was the only one in that immediate group who could answer his request.

For an instant, my mind gratefully flashed back five years to my Campus Crusade training time in Manila, when I had arrived there knowing no language but Khmer and French. Since the training was carried on in English, I knew my only hope of successful completion of the training was to learn English — quickly. Samoeun and I vowed to each other only to speak English to one another for the entire training time, and by the end of the six-month session I was able to teach some basic seminars in our newly-acquired language.

My English had become rusty in the last four years, as I had been quite mindful of its forbidden status in the Khmer Rouge's Cambodia. But I edged my way forward in the crowd anyway, and through the fence the reporter caught sight of my waving arm and heard my English greeting.

I went to the front of the crowd, and through the fence, my story tumbled out to the reporter, Michael Battye of Reuters News Agency, Thailand. I told him quickly of our life with the Khmer Rouge and then of my work with Campus Crusade. As I mentioned to him Campus Crusade, I pulled out my only means of identification: my Campus Crusade staff card which I had kept by faith, hoping for an opportunity such as this.

Mr. Battye scribbled my story hurriedly and took down my name and Samoeun's and Wiphousana's. On April 26, Battye sent the following story over the Reuters wire service:

ARANYAPRATHET, THAILAND, April 26 — The Thai army has transported more Campuchean (Cambodian) refugees to a mountain region south of this frontier town to join between 50,000 and 80,000 countrymen already there, informed sources said today. They said the new refugees, mostly civilians, were taken by trucks to the Kao Leong Mountains, which straddle the frontier about 30 miles south of here.

The Campucheans have been fleeing across the border into Thailand in the face of a fresh Vietnamese-led offensive by the new regime in Phnom Penh to crush opposition. Thai authorities have said that they would try to send the refugees back to their country as they had orders from the government not to allow them to stay in Thailand. . . . Among the refugees in the areas were 26 Campuchean Christians said by refugee officials to be only the third such group to escape to Thailand.

Vek Huong Taing, 30, told Reuters in a temporary refugee camp today that he had worked for the Manila-based Campus Crusade for Christ International before the Khmer Rouge took power four years ago.

He said that he and his wife had been forced to hide their religious beliefs during that period because discovery would have meant certain death.

On April 27, Mrs. Ethylyn Schultz, a staff member with Trans World Radio in Guam, was in the news room of the Agana radio station. She glanced down to the wire copy rolling onto the floor from the station's news teletype machine and her eyes caught the words, "Campus Crusade for Christ." Having been familiar with Campus Crusade already, she bent down to read the context. The story was Michael Battye's report. As soon as she read the story, Mrs. Schultz called Warren Willis, Campus Crusade's international representative in Guam.

Willis immediately telephoned Bailey Marks, the ministry's Asia-South Pacific director of affairs. Marks, who had never given up hope that we were alive, contacted Campus Crusade staff in Thailand to begin an urgent search for us, before repatriation efforts (by the Thai government) went into effect. Bangkok observers regarded return to Cambodia as almost certain death, especially for known Christians.

An immediate effort was then launched, both in Thailand and the United States, to locate us, secure our release from the camp and clear the way for us to come to America. In Thailand, Campus Crusade staff contacted the local authorities and the Refugee Section of the U.S. Embassy in Bangkok to win our release from the temporary refugee camp and to obtain visas to the U.S. In the States, U.S. Senator William Armstrong was contacted, who began working with the State Department Refugee Section. Campus Crusade staff, operating separately from Senator Armstrong, located reporter Battye in Bangkok, found out from him the name and location of our camp and turned the information over to the State Department on Sunday morning, April 29.

Less than 24 hours after Warren Willis' call to Bailey Marks, four Campus Crusade staff members began walking through the Taphraya camp looking for us. Barb Bolin, Charlie Culbertson, Greg Fallow and Jintana Chaowonglert had been scouting the camp for us for hours when they came upon several members of our group huddled together. They would have walked right past them, except that Samoeun, ever on the lookout, walked over to Charlie, who was wearing a *barong* (a Filipino shirt).

"I've seen that kind of shirt before," Samoeun said.

Charlie answered, "That's from the Philippines."

"I lived in the Philippines."

"What's your name?"

Samoeun moved closer and said "I'm Samoeun." Then Charlie held up a copy of a small yellow booklet published by Campus Crusade entitled, "Have You Heard of the Four Spiritual Laws?" Samoeun recognized it immediately and cried out with joy. She and Charlie embraced, with tears flowing freely.

A few minutes later, I came upon the scene, and when I joined in the celebration, our friends gave me a copy of the letter I had sent to Bailey Marks on April 7, 1975 telling him of our decision to stay in Cambodia. The letter had arrived in Manila several days after Cambodia's fall to the Khmer Rouge.

We remained in Taphraya for three more days, while arrangements were being made for our release. On May 1, only seven days after our group had arrived in Taphraya, we left our temporary home for Bangkok with another Campus Crusade staff member, Paul Utley. Just before I left the camp, I said a tearful goodbye to my 23 friends and 19 new believers. I asked them to pray and wait expectantly for God's special plan for them to be revealed.

Samoeun, Wiphousana and I then climbed into a car for the ride to Bangkok. It was our first ride in an automobile in four years, and the three of us fell victim to car-sickness! Fortunately, Charlie Culbertson and Paul were very understanding and stopped at the first store they could for some medicine before we resumed our trip.

When we arrived in Bangkok, I was hesitant to get out of the car, since I was wearing only a ragged shirt and a pair of shorts given to me by the Red Cross in Ta-phraya. Charlie quickly measured me and before I knew it, he had left and returned with a pair of just purchased long pants.

In Bangkok, we went to stay at another temporary camp for a couple of days while Paul Utley, Bailey Marks (who had just arrived) and another staff couple, Bud and Elizabeth Newbold, worked to process our visas. On May 4, a welcome party was given us by the whole Bangkok Campus Crusade staff, and that night we slept in a guest house of the Christian and Missionary Alliance.

That night was the first of my son's young life to sleep on a bed, since he was only two months old when we fled Phnom Penh. When he saw the bed he asked Samoeun, in his unique parlance, "Mommy, is this the bed of our Lord?" Samoeun answered him "yes," and he happily climbed in.

On May 5, we received our permission to leave for the United States, and late that day we arrived in San Francisco, Calif., from Bangkok. After resting in a San Francisco hotel overnight, we flew the next day into Ontario Airport near San Bernardino, Calif., where Campus Crusade's international headquarters is located. San Bernardino would be our new home until we determined our future plans. (Efforts were continuing to bring the remaining members of our border-crossing group to the United States also, and on June 27, they arrived safely in San Bernardino.)

When Samoeun and I stepped out of the plane at the Ontario Airport, a whole contingent of Campus Crusade staff and former American missionaries to Cambodia stood waving happily in greeting as we descended the plane's steps.

Our feeling as we stepped off the plane was indescribable: we could not believe that we were in America, being welcomed by spiritual brothers and sisters we had wondered if we'd ever see, and free once again to pursue our ministry. For a brief moment,

Samoeun and I discussed the wonder of it, and then we just thanked God from our hearts as our feet touched the California ground.

Epilogue

Epilogue

ORDEAL IN CAMBODIA

The population of Cambodia in 1975 was approximately seven million. In 1979, it was estimated at four million. The Khmer Rouge, through starvation, deprivation, torture and execution had cut Cambodia's population almost in half.

As I reflect back on my four years with the Khmer Rouge, I am amazed that Samoeun, Wiphousana and I are still alive. Pol Pot's regime put us through sufferings of every kind, and it was beyond our human capacity to have stood firm in the face of it all.

Many times I still think back on the innumerable sufferings — hunger, for example. How often I witnessed the agony of those dying by starvation, knowing that it is one of the worst ways for a human being to die. Even death by the gun was more welcome than starvation.

I often remember the deviously strategic use of hunger by the Khmer Rouge to insure their safety from the peoples' insurrection. I remember often being so hungry that I would secretly boil leaves of trees or long blades of grass to try to fill my stomach. And more than once I heard the last words of someone dying from starvation, "If I have rice, I will not die! Just give me one bowl and I will live!" The dying's last thoughts were not of family and friends — only of the wish for one life-saving bowl of rice.

I often think back, too, on the never-ending fear which was characteristic of Khmer Rouge existence. We worked hard day and night, and yet we could never please the Khmer Rouge. For us to live from day to day was to be like a bird in a cage, wanting to fly free. We never had a guarantee that any given day wouldn't bring death by execution. There was never a rest from wariness.

Samoeun and I, of all the people, were most qualified to have been killed. We could have been put to death for any one of six reasons: We were Christians. We were college graduates. We had worked for an American organization. We were from a large urban area. We had traveled out of the country before the fall. My brother, Chhirc, was a major in the deposed Lon Nol army. But we are alive today against all odds, and we feel this is our "second life."

During our four years in Cambodia, we learned many lessons. Some of these things we learned intellectually in the Campus Crusade training center in Manila, Philippines a year before the Khmer Rouge took over in Cambodia. But during the Khmer Rouge's rule, we learned these lessons in our experience. Six lessons among many stand out from this time.

Most dramatically I learned of the value of life and possessions on April 17, 1975, when the Khmer Rouge invaded Phnom Penh, and within 48 hours Samoeun and I owned nothing but the clothes on our backs and the few possessions we had stuffed in our car. Eventually, of course, we lost the car and its contents, and later on my watch and wedding band. Rarely, during our four years did Samoeun and I even have shoes for our feet. Money became useless. As Cambodia's factories and industries were laid to waste by the Khmer Rouge, and shops and markets were snuffed out of existence, currency lost its value, bringing to a halt, within a few days, an entire nation's economy.

Life itself became meaningless to Pol Pot's communists — April 17 also bearing proof of this when thousands of hospital patients perished along the roads leading out of Phnom Penh as the Khmer Rouge's mad scheme for ushering in a new society was mercilessly put into effect.

Our lives were considered even lower than animal life; sometimes Khmer Rouge soldiers would tell us that, when a cow died, they were very sorry, because it could no longer work the land. But if one of us died, in their eyes it was neither a gain nor a loss.

For many people under the vise of Khmer Rouge control, life eventually lost its value personally, and suicide became their only escape route. It was difficult in that environment to keep caring about oneself. Self-esteem was lost because of the total lack of provisions for maintaining personal bodily cleanliness and because of the pressures of accusations and fears of death.

I also learned through my four years

with the Khmer Rouge to live by faith. I learned that I must let God lead me step by step, placing my complete trust in His character of unspeakable love and goodness. Time and again, He proved to me that He is motivated in all things by love for me and is able to turn every situation into something that will glorify His name and help me become more like His Son, Jesus Christ.

I learned not to place pride or full confidence in my abilities to figure out solutions to the many problems we encountered. As God led us from village to village, there was no way I could have known the perfect timing of each move and of each circumstance surrounding those moves.

I learned not to worry about food and clothes. I remember reading Christ's words in Matthew 6, "Do not be anxious for your life, as to what you shall eat, or what you shall drink; nor for your body, as to what you shall put on. Is not life more than food, and the body clothing? Look at the birds of the air, that they do not sow, neither do they reap, nor gather into barns, and yet your heavenly Father feeds them. Are you not worth much more than they?" During my time in the jungles of Cambodia, I experienced the truth of these words.

God provided new clothes for us when we needed them, through Kheang's family in Norea, for instance. And though I did not have proper vitamins during the four years with the Khmer Rouge, nor did I once have meat — and vegetables only rarely — God gave me enough nutrients to generally keep me in good health and maintain my physical strength.

Finally, I learned simply to rest in God's plan. Many of the sufferings and obstacles I encountered, both physical and spiritual, caused me much fear. When I met those hard things, I often prayed, "Oh, Lord, I decided to live in Cambodia to serve You. Now I have no liberty, no possibilities, and no time to serve You. I suffer much for the communists but not for You. Why do You want me to have it like this? Why, God, why?"

Then God would restore peace to my heart as I remembered that my life is in His hands. He promised He would let me know His plan for my life step by step. As I look back and realize how He brought me into a place of liberty and freedom, I know that He

never once lost control of my life or circumstances.

Finally, I am painfully aware of the ex-
plosive state of the world today, and that the
time may be drawing short for people to con-
sider spiritual things. Had I not known
Christ, and had I not been focused on spiritual values, I would have been left without
hope or purpose during the four years I wandered in the jungles of Cambodia under the
Khmer Rouge.

Samoeun and I have decided that we are
fully committed to doing God's will in the
future, even if it should entail further suffering. Anywhere He wants to send us we will
go. We are ready to return to Cambodia to
serve our Lord Jesus if the doors are opened
once again for us to share our faith in Christ
there. Now, as we reside in the United
States, we want to continue carrying the
message of Christ's love to others, especially
to the thousands of Southeast Asian refugees like us being resettled here.

There is a song we learned from our
Campus Crusade training time in Manila.
Samoeun and I often sang it softly to ourselves as we worked in the fields. The first
line says, "This world is not my home . . ." I

130   pray that I will not forget the things God
taught me through the Khmer Rouge's
Cambodia, especially that His eternal values are all that will last in this life.

Chronology

April 7, 1975
LAST TELEGRAM
Huong Taing sent cable to Bailey Marks expressing his and his wife's commitment to stay in Cambodia and share Christ with their countrymen.

April 12, 1975
BOMBS AND PRAYER
Huong and Samoeun took 100 students to the outskirts of Phnom Penh for a day of Christian training. Training was interrupted as bombs dropped all around them. Huong instructed the students to open their Bibles to Psalm 91 and lie on the ground. They prayed through this passage as the bombs fell. Not one was hurt.

April 17, 1975
THE FALL OF PHNOM PENH
The day Phnom Penh fell. Huong and 30 students went into the street to share their faith in Jesus Christ, proclaiming "We want not only to live for Christ, but we will die for Him, too, if need be."

April 18, 1975
HARD LABOR
Ordered to leave the city. Went to Takoa. Huong was put in hard labor detail. Food was scarce. Many risked their lives to help feed Huong, Samoeun and their two-month-old son.

August, 1975
NORTH TO BATTAMBANG
Ordered to Battambang. At Pursat, a friendly Khmer Rouge soldier offered them a safe place to stay, but they turned down the offer of safety and boarded the train for Battambang.

August 15 - October, 1975
INTO THE FOREST
Kok Trom — forced out of the train into the forest, despite threatening storm. Spent the night in a makeshift shelter. The next day built a shelter for the family.

Huong caught one eight-inch fish each day in a rice paddy.

After two months, they went to the station to wait for a train to Battambang. They had no identification papers or passes.

A train full of Khmer Rouge soldiers pulled in. The same friendly soldier from Pursat was on board, recognized them, gave them the necessary passes — and they boarded — the *only* civilians on the train — without one word of challenge.

October, 1975 - September, 1976
UP THE COCONUT TREES
Ended up in Norea — after one night in Battambang. Here God gave Huong the ability to climb coconut trees — a very difficult skill. He became the main person the Khmer Rouge used to climb the coconut trees when coconuts were needed for food, medicine, etc.

Huong would climb the tree, throw down a number of coconuts and get one himself as payment.

131

Chronology

September - November, 1976
REQUESTED MURDER

A Chinese woman arranged for them to go to Watt Kor. When they thanked God for this provision, the woman got furious and charged them with being Christians and working with the Americans. She asked the chief to kill them.

Cheng Kdar was the next village on the way to Battambang. The Khmer Rouge were very strict there. The Taings were sent there.

November, 1976 - January, 1979
MORE THREAT OF DEATH

When they arrived in Cheng Kdar, they were asked for their story. They explained that they were Christians and had worked with Campus Crusade for Christ International. All this was taken down and sent to a higher authority.

Samoeun's work supervisor wanted to have her killed. Samoeun and Huong prayed daily for the woman to become a friend. In a few weeks, she became Samoeun's friend.

January, 1979
VIETNAMESE INVASION

Vietnamese invaded Cheng Kdar. The people fled to the mountains.

After the bombing stopped, the people in the mountains were afraid to go back to the village. Huong and some others decided to go back . . . the village was silent — just dead bodies.

The Taings walked on to Battambang, then to Sisophon — still closer to the Thai border.

February, 1979 - April 21, 1979
ESCAPE INTO THAILAND

They waited in Sisophon . . . very difficult to go over the mountains into Thailand — guides were needed to get through.

A woman paid $9,000 in gold to hire guides to lead them to the Thai border.

April 23, 1979
SAFE!

After four years, the Taings crossed safely into Thailand.

April 25, 1979
DISCOVERY

They were discovered in a refugee concentration camp by Reuters reporter Michael Battye who included their affiliation with Campus Crusade in an April 26 news story.

April 27, 1979
THE NEWS GETS OUT

A Trans World Radio staffer read the story and notified Campus Crusade staff in Guam. At 2:30 a.m. urgent moves began to secure the Taings' release from the camp.

May 7, 1979
FAMILY REUNION

The Taings arrived at the Ontario, Calif. airport, greeted by hundreds of people who had gathered to welcome them to the U.S.

July, 1979
A NEW HOME — A NEW LIFE

The Taings are now residing in their first home in over four years in San Bernardino, Calif.